Plants in My World

OUR FLOWER GARDEN

Dorothy Jennings

PowerKiDS press.

NEW YORK

Published in 2018 by The Rosen Publishing Group, Inc.
29 East 21st Street, New York, NY 10010

First Edition

Editor: Theresa Morlock
Book Design: Michael Flynn

Photo Credits: Cover Studio 37/Shutterstock.com; p. 5 Patrick Foto/Shutterstock.com; p. 6 Landscape Nature Photo/Shutterstock.com; p. 9 Ekaterina_Minaeva/Shutterstock.com; p. 10 canghai76/Shutterstock.com; p. 10 (inset) Sergii Votit /Shutterstock.com; p. 13 BENVALEE ONTHAWORN/Shutterstock.com; p. 14 SW Productions/Getty Images; p. 17 SrsPvl/Shutterstock.com; p. 19 Apimook/Shutterstock.com; p. 21 Ian Grainger/Getty Images; p. 22 AfricaImages/Getty Images.

Cataloging-in-Publication Data

Names: Jennings, Dorothy.
Title: Our flower garden / Dorothy Jennings.
Description: New York : PowerKids Press, 2018. | Series: Plants in my world | Includes index.
Identifiers: ISBN 9781538321171 (pbk.) | ISBN 9781538321188 (library bound) | ISBN 9781508161721 (6 pack)
Subjects: LCSH: Flower gardening–Juvenile literature.
Classification: LCC SB406.5 J46 2018 | DDC 635.9–dc23

Manufactured in China

CPSIA Compliance Information: Batch #BS17PK: For Further Information contact Rosen Publishing, New York, New York at 1-800-237-9932

Please visit: www.rosenpublishing.com and www.habausa.com

CONTENTS

Many Sizes

Flowers come in all shapes and sizes.

Sunflowers are tall, and so are lupines.

Buttercups are short, and so are forget-me-nots.

There are so many kinds to see!

Beautiful Colors

Flowers can be different colors. Marigolds can be red or orange. Lilacs can be purple, pink, or white. Tulips can be purple, pink, red, orange, or yellow!

Flowers have blossoms, leaves, stems, and roots. Roots reach into the ground and keep the flower steady. A flower's stem grows up. Flower stems and leaves are green.

poppies

peonies

Blossoms are made of parts called petals. Some flowers have lots of petals and others have just a few. A peony has rows and rows of petals. A poppy has just four petals.

Some flowers grow on a vine. A vine is a kind of stem that climbs by winding itself around things. Morning glories climb as high as they can! You might see them on a fence or a wall.

What They Need

Like all plants, flowers need water, sunshine, and healthy soil. They also need a gas called carbon dioxide. Plants use sunlight to turn water and carbon dioxide into food.

Flowers don't just grow in our gardens. They grow in meadows, mountains, and forests. They grow on the branches of trees. Some even grow in water!

Sweet Nectar

Flowers make sweet nectar. Bees, hummingbirds, and butterflies drink nectar. These creatures brush against the flowers and spread their pollen. Pollen is what a flower needs to make more flowers.

People give each other flowers for special events, such as birthdays. Flowers can cheer someone up when they're not feeling well. The flowers you grow in your garden can make people happy.

Flowers fill the world with beauty. Their bright colors and sweet smells brighten our planet and give people joy. You can plant your very own flower garden too!

WORDS TO KNOW

petals

roots

stem

INDEX